Read-About Science

Cactuses

By Allan Fowler

Consultants

Martha Walsh, Reading Specialist

Jan Jenner, Ph.D

Children's Press®
A Division of Scholastic Inc.
New York   Toronto   London   Auckland   Sydney
Mexico City   New Delhi   Hong Kong
Danbury, Connecticut

Designer: Herman Adler Design
Photo Researcher: Caroline Anderson
The photo on the cover shows prickly pear cactuses growing in Arizona.

Library of Congress Cataloging-in-Publication Data

Fowler, Allan.
    Cactuses / by Allan Fowler.
      p. cm. — (Rookie read-about science)
    Includes index.
    Summary: This introductory book discusses the different kinds of
cactuses and where they grow.
    ISBN 0-516-21686-4 (lib. bdg.)   0-516-25983-0 (pbk.)
    1. Cactus—Juvenile literature. [1. Cactus.] I. Title. II. Series.
QK495.C11 F67   2001
583'.56—dc21

                          00-055572

Most plants need good soil
and plenty of water to grow.

But cactuses grow in dry
places, such as deserts.

Sand and rocks cover
most deserts. Very little
rain falls there.

Cactuses grow in the deserts of the southwestern United States.

They are also found in Mexico, Central America, and South America.

Roots

8

Cactuses have long roots that grow near the surface, or top, of the ground.

Cactuses use their roots to drink rainwater. They keep the water inside their stems for a long time.

Cactuses come in different shapes and sizes.

Some stand straight up like trees. Branches grow out of their stems.

Other cactuses have
flat stems shaped like
Ping-Pong paddles.

This plant is called a barrel cactus because of its shape.

14

Almost all cactuses have sharp spines. The spines keep animals from eating them.

Flowers grow on some cactus plants.

These flowers can be
very colorful.

Some cactus plants grow edible fruit. Edible means you can safely eat them.

This is a prickly pear cactus.

Its tasty fruit is shaped like a pear with bumps.

You can also eat the fruit
of a saguaro (sa–GWA–ro).
It is the tallest cactus.

Some saguaros grow to be sixty feet tall. They can have more than twenty branches.

Saguaros grow in the
Sonoran Desert of Arizona
and northern Mexico.

The saguaro blossom is
Arizona's state flower.

Small cactuses make good houseplants. People like their different shapes.

You do not have to water
a cactus very often.

But watch your fingers!
Those spines are very sharp.

Words You Know

barrel cactus

flowers

fruit

prickly pear

roots

saguaro

spines

31

Index

About the Author

Allan Fowler is a freelance writer with a background in advertising. Born in New York, he now lives in Chicago and enjoys traveling.

Photo Credits